RETURN TO THE GOSPEL

A Clarion Call to return to the Message
the Apostles Preached

Jacob Biswell

Cover design by Jacob Biswell
Interior design by S.I. Book Interiors
Printed in the United States of America
ISBN: 979-8-9990264-2-2
First Edition

Disclaimer

Artificial Intelligence (AI) tools were utilized in the editing and design process of this book. The interior text was edited with the assistance of AI for clarity and flow; however, all ideas, theology, and original thoughts are entirely those of the author. The cover artwork was designed with the help of AI, guided by the author's original vision and direction.

TABLE OF CONTENTS

Introduction

THE SOUND OF THE CLARION

There is a sound in the Spirit—a clarion call echoing across the nations and reverberating through the Church. It is not the sound of novelty, nor of the latest spiritual trend, nor of the noise of competing ideologies. It is the ancient sound, the trumpet blast of God, summoning His people to return to the Gospel the Apostles preached[1].

The Gospel that turned the world upside down[2] has, in many places, been reduced to a set of inspirational slogans, moralistic platitudes, or consumer-driven promises of personal success. What the Apostles proclaimed as the power of God unto salvation[3]—rooted in the story of Israel[4], centered on Christ crucified and risen[5], crowned with eschatological hope[6]—has been replaced in many pulpits by messages that soothe rather than save, entertain rather than equip, and appease rather than awaken[7].

This book is not an academic exercise in nostalgia. It is a prophetic cry. We stand at a critical juncture in the history of the Church and the world. The signs of the times press upon us: nations in turmoil[8], moral confusion[9], wars and rumors of wars[10], and the increasing marginalization of biblical truth[11]. In such an hour, only the true Gospel—the Gospel the Apostles preached—can anchor the Church and advance the Kingdom[12].

What was this Gospel? It was not merely "how to get to heaven when you die." It was the announcement that Jesus of Nazareth, the crucified

One, is both Lord and Christ[13]. It was the declaration that in Him, the promises made to the fathers of Israel have been fulfilled[14]. It was the proclamation that He has risen from the dead[15], ascended to the right hand of God[16], and will return to judge the living and the dead[17], to restore all things[18], and to reign from Jerusalem over all nations[19].

The Apostolic Gospel was rooted in the soil of Israel's story[20]. It was and remains inseparable from the covenant faithfulness of God to His people Israel[21] and His plan for the restoration of all creation[22]. To preach the Gospel apart from Israel is to preach an amputated Gospel[23]. To proclaim Christ without His coming Kingdom is to offer a half-truth that leaves the Church unprepared for the hour at hand[24].

This book is a call to return—to the message that first shook empires and transformed hearts. It is a summons to re-center our preaching, teaching, and living on the Gospel that announces:

- The King has come, He has conquered sin and death, and He will come again[25].

- God's covenant with Israel has not failed but is being fulfilled in Christ and will culminate in Israel's restoration and the renewal of all things[26].

- The Gospel is the power of God—not only to forgive sin but to create a people who live in light of His coming reign[27].

In these pages, we will journey through what the Apostles preached, how the Church has drifted, and how we can return. We will recover the Gospel as the Apostles knew it: a Gospel of the Kingdom, the cross, the resurrection, the return of Christ, and the restoration of Israel.

Let the trumpet blast awaken us[28]. The time is short[29]. The Bridegroom is at the door[30]. The nations are in the valley of decision[31]. And the Spirit is calling:

Return to the Gospel.

Endnotes

1. Jeremiah 6:16; Isaiah 58:1
2. Acts 17:6
3. Romans 1:16
4. Acts 13:32-33
5. 1 Corinthians 1:23; 1 Corinthians 15:3-4
6. Titus 2:13; 2 Peter 3:13
7. 2 Timothy 4:3-4
8. Matthew 24:6-7
9. Isaiah 5:20
10. Matthew 24:6
11. 2 Timothy 3:1-5
12. Hebrews 6:19; Matthew 24:14
13. Acts 2:36
14. Acts 13:32-33; Romans 15:8
15. Acts 2:32; 1 Corinthians 15:4
16. Acts 2:33; Hebrews 1:3
17. Acts 17:31; 2 Timothy 4:1
18. Acts 3:21
19. Isaiah 2:2-4; Zechariah 14:9; Acts 1:6-11
20. Romans 9:4-5
21. Jeremiah 31:35-37; Romans 11:1-2, 11-12, 25-29
22. Romans 8:19-23; Isaiah 11:6-9
23. Romans 11:18-21
24. Matthew 25:1-13; Revelation 19:7
25. Revelation 1:5-7; 1 Corinthians 15:25-26
26. Romans 11:25-27; Acts 3:19-21; Matthew 19:28
27. Titus 2:11-14; 1 Peter 2:9-12
28. Joel 2:1
29. Romans 13:11-12
30. Matthew 24:33
31. Joel 3:14

Chapter 1

THE GOSPEL OF THE KINGDOM AND THE KING OF ISRAEL

A Gospel Rooted in a Story, Not an Abstraction

The Gospel did not emerge in a vacuum. It did not fall from heaven as a set of isolated spiritual truths detached from history, covenant, or peoplehood. The Gospel that the Apostles preached was born out of the soil of Israel's sacred story—a story stretching back to the call of Abraham, the covenant at Sinai, the promise to David, the cries of the prophets, and the aching hope of a people longing for deliverance.

Paul opens his great epistle to the Romans by declaring that he was "set apart for the gospel of God, which He promised beforehand through His prophets in the holy Scriptures, concerning His Son, who was born of a descendant of David according to the flesh, who was declared the Son of God with power by the resurrection from the dead" (Rom. 1:1–4 NASB 1995). The Gospel is the fulfillment of God's promises to Israel. It is not new in its essence, though its realization in Christ is glorious beyond what the prophets could fully see.

When the Apostles preached, they did not begin with abstract spiritual needs. They began with the God of Israel, His covenant faithfulness, and His Messiah. Peter's sermon at Pentecost is a model of this apostolic proclamation. He anchors his message in Joel's prophecy of the outpouring of the Spirit, in David's promise of an everlasting King, and in the testimony of the resurrection as the vindication of Jesus' claim to be that King (Acts 2:14–36). The Gospel is the announcement that Israel's King has come, and in Him, the nations find their hope.

The Kingdom Has Come—But Its Fullness Awaits

Throughout His earthly ministry, Jesus announced: "Repent, for the kingdom of heaven is at hand" (Matt. 4:17). His miracles, His parables, His authority over demons, sickness, and nature were signs of the Kingdom's arrival. The blind saw, the lame walked, the dead were raised, and the poor heard good news (Matt. 11:5)—all signals that Israel's God was acting decisively.

Yet, the Kingdom came in a mystery. The expectation of many in Israel was for a political deliverer who would overthrow Rome and restore the throne of David immediately. Jesus did come to establish David's throne—but by a path few anticipated: the way of the cross. His Kingdom arrived like a mustard seed, small and hidden, destined to grow and fill the earth (Matt. 13:31-32). It came as leaven, silently working its transforming power (Matt. 13:33).

The Kingdom was inaugurated in Jesus' first coming. It is being extended through His Spirit-empowered Church. And it will be consummated at His return, when the kingdoms of this world will become the Kingdom of our Lord and of His Christ (Rev. 11:15).

To preach the Gospel apart from this Kingdom framework is to preach a truncated Gospel. The Apostles preached a Kingdom Gospel: Jesus is Lord. He reigns. His reign will one day fill the earth.

The Scandal of the Cross

The cross was not an unexpected accident in God's plan. It was the climactic moment in the story of Israel's redemption and the redemption of the world. As Paul boldly proclaimed: "We preach Christ crucified, to Jews a stumbling block and to Gentiles foolishness, but to those who are the called, both Jews and Greeks, Christ the power of God and the wisdom of God" (1 Cor. 1:23–24).

Why was the cross a stumbling block? Because it seemed to contradict the very hope of Israel—a Messiah who would reign, not one who would die in shame. The cross was Rome's instrument of public humiliation. Yet, in God's wisdom, it became the throne from which Jesus triumphed over sin, death, and Satan (Col. 2:14–15).

The cross is the center of the apostolic Gospel. Not as a mere example of love, but as the altar on which the Lamb of God took away the sins of the world (John 1:29). The blood of Jesus establishes the new covenant promised in Jeremiah 31. It secures forgiveness, restores relationship, and inaugurates the age to come.

The Resurrection: God's Declaration of Victory

The resurrection was not simply a happy ending to a tragic story. It was God's declaration to the world that Jesus is both Lord and Messiah (Acts 2:36). The resurrection vindicated His claims, fulfilled the Scriptures, and demonstrated that God's new creation had begun (1 Cor. 15:20–23).

In raising Jesus from the dead, God gave us the firstfruits of the age to come. The resurrection is eschatological—it points to the future renewal of all things, the redemption of our bodies, and the restoration of the world (Rom. 8:19–23). The Gospel the Apostles preached was filled with resurrection hope. It was a call to live in light of the coming day when death would be swallowed up in victory (1 Cor. 15:54).

Israel's Restoration and the Gospel

The Apostolic Gospel never forgot Israel. Even after the resurrection, the disciples asked, "Lord, is it at this time You are restoring the kingdom to Israel?" (Acts 1:6). Their hope was not misplaced. Jesus affirmed the restoration but placed its timing in the Father's hands (Acts 1:7).

Paul, writing decades later, speaks of the mystery of Israel's partial hardening and future salvation (Rom. 11:25–27). The Gospel is for the Jew first, and also for the Gentile (Rom. 1:16). The restoration of Israel is not a side note to the Gospel. It is part of the unfolding plan of God, as He brings all things under the headship of Christ (Eph. 1:10).

The Gospel anticipates the day when the Deliverer will come from Zion and remove ungodliness from Jacob. The Church must recover this vision—not as a political program, but as a theological and eschatological reality that shapes our mission and our hope.

A Prophetic Challenge for Our Generation

In our day, the Gospel has too often been reduced to a message of personal improvement, therapeutic comfort, or moralistic striving. The Kingdom has been postponed to the distant future, or spiritualized beyond recognition. The cross has been softened. The resurrection has been treated as a symbol rather than a reality. And Israel's place in God's purposes has been neglected, denied, or distorted.

But the trumpet blast is sounding. The Spirit is calling the Church to return. Return to the Gospel of the Kingdom. Return to the proclamation of Jesus as Lord of Israel and the nations. Return to the cross and the resurrection as the power of God. Return to the hope of His coming, the restoration of Israel, and the renewal of all things.

This is the Gospel the Apostles preached. This is the Gospel that will once again shake the nations and prepare the way for the King.

Endnotes

1. Romans 1:1–4
2. Acts 2:14–36
3. Genesis 12:1–3
4. 2 Samuel 7:12–16
5. Isaiah 49:6; Amos 9:11–12; Acts 15:15–17
6. Zechariah 14:9; Isaiah 2:2–4
7. Matthew 4:17
8. Luke 11:20; Colossians 1:13
9. Isaiah 53
10. Mark 3:27
11. Colossians 2:14–15
12. 1 Corinthians 15:20
13. 1 Corinthians 15:24–28; Revelation 11:15
14. 1 Corinthians 1:23–24
15. Colossians 2:15
16. Acts 2:36
17. Acts 1:6–7
18. Acts 1:7
19. Acts 1:8; Matthew 24:14
20. Romans 11:25–27
21. Romans 8:19–23; Isaiah 2:2–4; Zechariah 14:9
22. 2 Timothy 4:3–4
23. Matthew 25:1–13; Titus 2:13
24. Revelation 1:5–7; 1 Corinthians 15:25
25. Matthew 3:2; Mark 1:15
26. Habakkuk 2:14; Isaiah 11:9

Chapter 2

THE CROSS AT THE CENTER

The Cross: The Heart of the Apostolic Gospel

The cross is not peripheral to the Gospel. It is its blazing center. In a world obsessed with strength, power, and honor, the Apostles proclaimed the scandal of a crucified Messiah. The cross is not merely an unfortunate instrument of Jesus' death; it is the place where God's justice and mercy meet, where sin is condemned, where Satan is defeated, and where love is revealed in its purest form[1].

Paul summarized the Gospel he received and preached with these words:

"For I delivered to you as of first importance what I also received, that Christ died for our sins according to the Scriptures, and that He was buried, and that He was raised on the third day according to the Scriptures" (1 Cor. 15:3–4).

At the heart of this Gospel is the declaration that Christ died for our sins—a substitutionary, sacrificial death that fulfills the ancient promises and satisfies divine justice.

The Scandal and Power of the Cross

In the Roman world, the cross was a symbol of shame. Crucifixion was reserved for the worst criminals, rebels, and slaves. It was designed to humiliate as much as to kill. That is why the message of a crucified

King seemed absurd both to Jews, who expected a triumphant Messiah, and to Gentiles, who revered power and despised weakness[2].

Yet Paul boldly declared:

"But we preach Christ crucified, to Jews a stumbling block and to Gentiles foolishness, but to those who are the called, both Jews and Greeks, Christ the power of God and the wisdom of God" (1 Cor. 1:23–24).

The cross is the wisdom of God because through it He accomplished what human wisdom could never achieve: redemption, reconciliation, and victory over sin and death.

The Cross in Israel's Story

The Apostolic Gospel places the cross within the framework of Israel's story. The sacrificial system pointed to it. The Passover lamb anticipated it. The suffering servant of Isaiah 53 described it in haunting detail:

"But He was pierced through for our transgressions, He was crushed for our iniquities; the chastening for our well-being fell upon Him, and by His scourging we are healed" (Isa. 53:5).

On the cross, Jesus bore the curse of the Law (Gal. 3:13). He fulfilled the Day of Atonement by offering His own blood for the sins of the people (Heb. 9:12). He became the true and final sacrifice, ending the need for the blood of bulls and goats (Heb. 10:4–10).

The cross is not an abstract spiritual principle. It is the fulfillment of God's covenantal plan of redemption through Israel for the sake of the whole world[3].

The Cosmic Victory of the Cross

The Apostolic Gospel proclaims that through the cross, Christ triumphed over the cosmic powers of darkness. As Paul writes:

"When He had disarmed the rulers and authorities, He made a public display of them, having triumphed over them through Him [or it—meaning the cross]" (Col. 2:15).

What seemed like defeat was in fact the greatest victory. The cross is the decisive moment in the war against Satan. Sin's penalty is paid, death's power is broken, and the principalities and powers are exposed as impotent before the wisdom of God.

The Gospel is not only about personal forgiveness—it is the announcement of Christ's cosmic victory and the inauguration of His reign.

The Cross and the New Covenant

Jesus said at the Last Supper:

"This cup, which is poured out for you, is the new covenant in My blood" (Luke 22:20).

The cross establishes the new covenant promised in Jeremiah 31—a covenant in which God forgives sins, writes His law on our hearts, and brings His people into intimate relationship with Himself.

The Apostolic Gospel is covenantal. It proclaims that through the cross, God has acted decisively to forgive, cleanse, and restore. This covenant is offered first to the house of Israel and the house of Judah, and through them, extended to the nations (Jer. 31:31–34; Acts 3:25–26).

The Cross and the Call to Follow

The Apostolic Gospel does not stop at proclaiming Christ crucified for us. It calls us to take up our cross and follow Him. Jesus declared:

"If anyone wishes to come after Me, he must deny himself, and take up his cross daily and follow Me" (Luke 9:23).

The cross is both our salvation and our pattern. The Apostolic message invites us not only to believe in the cross but to live in its power—to die to sin, self, and the world, and to live for Christ (Gal. 2:20).

A Gospel without the call to the cross is not the Gospel the Apostles preached.

The Drift: Cross-less Christianity

In much of the modern Church, the cross has been sidelined. In its place, we have offered therapeutic messages that soothe but do not save. We have presented Christianity as a path to personal fulfillment rather than a call to die and rise with Christ.

The Apostles preached a Gospel that demanded repentance, confronted sin, and pointed to the cross as the only hope for a guilty world. We must return to this message if we are to see true awakening.

A Call to Return

The cross must be at the center of our preaching, our worship, our lives. We must proclaim:

- Christ crucified as our substitute and sacrifice.
- The cross as God's victory over sin, death, and Satan.
- The cross as the foundation of the new covenant.
- The cross as the pattern of discipleship.

When we return to the cross, we return to the power of God (1 Cor. 1:18). Only a cross-centered Gospel can produce a cross-shaped people who live for the glory of the crucified and risen King.

Endnotes

1. 1 Corinthians 15:3–4

2. 1 Corinthians 1:23–24

3. Isaiah 53; Hebrews 9:12–28; Galatians 3:13

Chapter 3

THE RESURRECTION AND THE HOPE OF GLORY

The Resurrection: The Seal of the Apostolic Gospel

The resurrection of Jesus Christ is the cornerstone of the Gospel. Without it, the message of the cross would remain a tragic tale of a martyred teacher, and our faith would be empty, powerless, and false. As Paul declared with unflinching clarity:

"If Christ has not been raised, your faith is worthless; you are still in your sins. Then those also who have fallen asleep in Christ have perished. If we have hoped in Christ in this life only, we are of all men most to be pitied" (1 Cor. 15:17–19 NASB 1995).

But Christ has been raised! The resurrection is God's declaration to the world that Jesus is the Son of God in power, the Messiah of Israel, and the Lord of heaven and earth (Rom. 1:4). The empty tomb is the Father's vindication of the Son's obedience, the public announcement that death has been defeated, and the firstfruits of a new creation that will one day flood the earth with life.

The Resurrection in Israel's Hope

The Apostolic Gospel did not proclaim resurrection as a vague spiritual metaphor or mystical experience. It declared a real, bodily resurrection, in continuity with the hope of Israel's prophets.

Daniel foresaw a day when "many of those who sleep in the dust of the ground will awake, these to everlasting life, but the others to disgrace and everlasting contempt" (Dan. 12:2).

Isaiah promised: "Your dead will live; their corpses will rise. You who lie in the dust, awake and shout for joy" (Isa. 26:19).

The resurrection of Jesus is the beginning of that promised restoration. It is the guarantee that God will do for the whole creation what He has already done for Jesus (Rom. 8:19–23). The tomb could not hold Him, and one day, the grave will release all who belong to Him.

The Apostolic Gospel preached the resurrection as the dawn of the age to come. It announced that the powers of the old age—sin, death, and Satan—had been broken, and that a new world had begun in Christ.

The Resurrection as Vindication

In raising Jesus from the dead, God overturned the verdict of human courts. The rulers of this age condemned Him as a blasphemer and a rebel; God declared Him to be Lord and Christ (Acts 2:36).

Peter, on Pentecost, boldly proclaimed:

"This Jesus God raised up again, to which we are all witnesses... Therefore let all the house of Israel know for certain that God has made Him both Lord and Christ—this Jesus whom you crucified" (Acts 2:32, 36).

The resurrection is God's "Amen" to all that Jesus said and did. It is the assurance that His sacrifice was accepted, His mission accomplished, His identity confirmed. Without the resurrection, there is no assurance that sin is atoned for or that death is defeated.

The Resurrection and the Kingdom

The Apostolic Gospel links the resurrection to the coming reign of God. The resurrection of Jesus is the beginning of His rule:

"For He must reign until He has put all His enemies under His feet. The last enemy that will be abolished is death" (1 Cor. 15:25–26).

His resurrection enthroned Him as the Davidic King promised by the prophets (Ps. 110:1; Acts 2:34–35). From His exalted position at the right hand of God, He now rules, extending His Kingdom through His Spirit-empowered Church, until the day He returns to bring that rule in fullness.

The resurrection is not merely about life after death; it is about the victory of the Kingdom of God over the powers of darkness and the establishment of God's righteous rule over the nations.

The Resurrection and the Restoration of All Things

When Peter preached at the temple after healing the lame man, he connected the resurrection to the final restoration:

"Therefore repent and return, so that your sins may be wiped away, in order that times of refreshing may come from the presence of the Lord; and that He may send Jesus, the Christ appointed for you, whom heaven must receive until the period of restoration of all things about which God spoke by the mouth of His holy prophets from ancient time" (Acts 3:19–21).

The resurrection is the guarantee that God will fulfill His promises—to Israel, to creation, to the nations. It is the firstfruits of the age to come, when every tear will be wiped away, and death will be no more (Rev. 21:4).

The Apostolic Gospel proclaims a hope that is cosmic in scope. The resurrection assures us that God's purpose is not to abandon the world, but to redeem it.

The Drift: Resurrection Forgotten or Reimagined

In much of the modern Church, the resurrection has been reduced to a symbol of hope or a metaphor for personal renewal. The historic, bodily resurrection of Jesus is often sidelined, and the future hope of bodily resurrection for His people is neglected in favor of vague notions of "going to heaven when we die."

But the Apostolic Gospel proclaims resurrection life now, and resurrection glory to come. The Apostles called the Church to live as those who have been raised with Christ (Col. 3:1), to set our hope fully on the grace to be revealed at His coming (1 Pet. 1:13), and to long for the day when our bodies will be raised in glory (Phil. 3:20–21).

We must recover this resurrection hope if we are to be the Church that proclaims the Gospel the Apostles preached.

A Call to Return

The resurrection is the foundation of Christian hope. It is the assurance that Christ reigns, that sin is conquered, that death is doomed, and that glory awaits.

To return to the Apostolic Gospel is to proclaim:

- Christ has been raised, the firstfruits of those who sleep.

- Death has lost its sting; the grave has lost its victory.

- A new creation has begun, and we are its citizens, called to live in its power and hope.

Let us lift our eyes from earthly distractions and fix them on the risen Christ. Let us preach the resurrection, live in its power, and long for the day when we will see Him face to face.

Endnotes

1. 1 Corinthians 15:17–19
2. Romans 1:4
3. Daniel 12:2; Isaiah 26:19
4. Romans 8:19–23
5. Acts 2:32, 36
6. 1 Corinthians 15:25–26
7. Acts 3:19–21
8. Revelation 21:4
9. Colossians 3:1
10. 1 Peter 1:13
11. Philippians 3:20–21

Chapter 4

THE COMING KING AND THE CONSUMMATION

The Apostolic Gospel Points Forward

The Gospel the Apostles preached was not only a declaration of what Christ had done—it was a proclamation of what Christ will do. The crucified, risen, and ascended King will come again in glory to judge the living and the dead, to reign upon the earth, and to restore all things according to the promise of God[1]. The Gospel is incomplete without this forward-looking hope. The return of Christ is not a footnote to the Gospel; it is its climax.

The Apostolic Gospel proclaimed that history is not aimless. It is moving toward a glorious consummation:

"He has fixed a day in which He will judge the world in righteousness through a Man whom He has appointed, having furnished proof to all men by raising Him from the dead" (Acts 17:31 NASB 1995).

The Promise of His Return

The return of Jesus was not a peripheral teaching in apostolic preaching. It was at the heart of their hope, their message, and their mission. When Jesus ascended, the angels declared to the watching disciples:

"Men of Galilee, why do you stand looking into the sky? This Jesus, who has been taken up from you into heaven, will come in just the same way as you have watched Him go into heaven" (Acts 1:11).

The Apostolic Gospel is the announcement that the risen Jesus is coming again—personally, bodily, and gloriously. His coming will be visible, unmistakable, and victorious (Matt. 24:27–30; Rev. 1:7). The King will return to reign from Zion (Isa. 2:2–4; Zech. 14:9), to judge the nations (Matt. 25:31–46), and to restore creation (Acts 3:21).

The Restoration of Israel

From the beginning of the apostolic mission, the restoration of Israel was seen as part of the unfolding plan of God. Even after the resurrection, the disciples asked, "Lord, is it at this time You are restoring the kingdom to Israel?" (Acts 1:6). This was not an error of misplaced nationalism. It was the natural expectation of those who knew the promises of the prophets.

Jesus did not deny the hope; He deferred its timing to the Father's authority (Acts 1:7). But He affirmed the mission: to bear witness to Him to the ends of the earth (Acts 1:8), until the day when the Deliverer would come from Zion and all Israel would be saved (Rom. 11:25–27).

The return of Christ will bring the fulfillment of God's covenant promises to Israel, not in place of His promises to the nations, but in their completion. The restoration of Israel and the renewal of the nations are inseparably bound together in the Gospel the Apostles preached.

The Consummation of the Kingdom

The Apostolic Gospel proclaims that the Kingdom has come in Christ's first coming, is advancing through the Church by the Spirit, and will be consummated at His return. Paul declared:

"Then comes the end, when He hands over the kingdom to the God and Father, when He has abolished all rule and all authority and power. For He must reign until He has put all His enemies under His feet. The last enemy that will be abolished is death" (1 Cor. 15:24–26).

At His coming, Christ will destroy His enemies, including death itself. He will reign upon the earth, and the glory of the Lord will cover the earth as the waters cover the sea (Hab. 2:14). The meek will inherit the earth (Matt. 5:5), and the nations will stream to Zion to learn His ways (Isa. 2:3).

The New Creation

The coming of Christ will bring about not only the restoration of Israel and the consummation of the Kingdom but also the renewal of all creation. The Apostolic Gospel points to the day when:

"He who sits on the throne said, 'Behold, I am making all things new'" (Rev. 21:5).

The earth, now groaning under the weight of sin, will be set free from its corruption (Rom. 8:19–21). The curse will be lifted (Rev. 22:3). Death, mourning, crying, and pain will be no more (Rev. 21:4). The new Jerusalem will descend, and God will dwell with His people forever.

This is the hope of glory that the Apostolic Gospel holds forth. It is not escapism, but the promise of God's victory and renewal.

The Drift: A Gospel Without the King's Return

In many places today, the Gospel has been truncated. The return of Christ is treated as a distant doctrine for theologians and prophecy buffs rather than as the centerpiece of Christian hope. Some have so over-spiritualized the Kingdom that they have no place left for the King's physical return. Others have replaced the hope of His appearing with dreams of political solutions or human progress.

But the Apostolic Gospel calls us back. It declares that history is His story. The King will come. Justice will be done. The meek will inherit the earth. The promise will be fulfilled.

A Call to Return

The clarion call of the Spirit in this hour is to return to the Gospel that proclaims:

- Christ will come again in glory.
- The Kingdom will be consummated in His reign upon the earth.
- Israel will be restored, and the nations will worship the King.
- Creation will be renewed, and righteousness will dwell.

This is the Gospel the Apostles preached. This is the Gospel that gives hope, demands holiness, and fuels mission. Let us live in its light. Let us proclaim it with boldness. Let us long for His appearing.

Endnotes

1. Acts 17:31
2. Acts 1:11
3. Matthew 24:27–30; Revelation 1:7
4. Isaiah 2:2–4; Zechariah 14:9
5. Matthew 25:31–46
6. Acts 3:21
7. Romans 11:25–27
8. 1 Corinthians 15:24–26
9. Habakkuk 2:14
10. Matthew 5:5
11. Revelation 21:4–5
12. Romans 8:19–21

Chapter 5

THE CALL TO REPENTANCE, FAITH, BAPTISM, AND THE SPIRIT – AND AWAIT HIS RETURN

The Gospel Demands a Response

The Apostolic Gospel was never proclaimed as a set of abstract truths for intellectual assent. It was a summons—a divine call demanding a decisive response. When the Apostles preached, they did not merely present information; they issued an invitation and a warning:

"Repent, and each of you be baptized in the name of Jesus Christ for the forgiveness of your sins; and you will receive the gift of the Holy Spirit" (Acts 2:38 NASB 1995).

The Gospel that announces the Kingdom, the cross, the resurrection, and the coming reign of Christ calls all people everywhere to turn, believe, submit, and await the return of the King. It is not a passive message. It is an urgent call: Repent, believe, be baptized, be filled, and live in joyful expectancy.

Repentance: Turning to the King

The first word of the Gospel is Repent. John the Baptist began his ministry with this cry (Matt. 3:2). Jesus began His preaching the same way (Matt. 4:17). And the Apostles continued the call:

"Therefore having overlooked the times of ignorance, God is now declaring to men that all people everywhere should repent" (Acts 17:30).

Repentance is not mere remorse. It is a radical turning—from sin to God, from idols to the living God, from self-rule to Christ's lordship. It involves a change of mind that leads to a change of life (Acts 26:20). Repentance humbles the sinner before God, confesses His justice, and embraces His mercy. It is the necessary doorway to the Kingdom (Luke 13:3, 5).

Faith: Allegiance to the King

The Apostolic Gospel calls for faith—not as passive intellectual agreement, but as wholehearted trust, surrender, and allegiance to Jesus as the risen Lord. Paul declared:

"If you confess with your mouth Jesus as Lord, and believe in your heart that God raised Him from the dead, you will be saved" (Rom. 10:9).

Faith clings to Jesus for forgiveness, hopes in Him for resurrection, and submits to Him in obedience (Rom. 1:5; Gal. 2:20). It is the active loyalty of the heart awakened by grace.

Baptism: Identification with the King

The Apostolic Gospel joins repentance and faith with the public act of baptism. On Pentecost, those who received the word were baptized (Acts 2:41). The Ethiopian eunuch asked, "What prevents me from being baptized?" (Acts 8:36). The Philippian jailer and his household were baptized the same night (Acts 16:33).

Baptism is not a human tradition or empty rite. It is God's appointed sign of entry into Christ's body, the Church (1 Cor. 12:13). It symbolizes union with Christ in His death, burial, and resurrection (Rom. 6:3–4). It is the pledge of a good conscience toward God (1 Pet. 3:21). It publicly declares that Jesus alone is Lord.

The Baptism of the Holy Spirit: Empowered for the King's Mission

The Apostolic Gospel does not stop at forgiveness. It proclaims the promise of the Spirit's power. Jesus commanded:

"Wait for what the Father has promised… for John baptized with water, but you will be baptized with the Holy Spirit not many days from now" (Acts 1:4–5).

"You will receive power when the Holy Spirit has come upon you; and you shall be My witnesses" (Acts 1:8).

The Baptism of the Holy Spirit is not a private mystical experience. It is the empowering presence of God for mission, holiness, and Kingdom demonstration. The Spirit is the seal of the new covenant (Acts 2:38–39; Joel 2:28–29; Ezek. 36:25–27). The Spirit's power clothes the Church for witness, confirming the word with signs following (Mark 16:20).

A Life of Watchful Hope

The Apostolic Gospel does not stop at the initial response. It calls for a life lived in expectation:

"We wait for His Son from heaven, whom He raised from the dead, that is Jesus, who rescues us from the wrath to come" (1 Thess. 1:10).

This hope inspires holiness (1 John 3:2–3), fuels mission (Matt. 24:14), and sustains endurance in suffering (Rom. 8:18). The Church lives between the cross and the crown, between Pentecost and the Parousia.

The Drift — And the Call to Return

Much of the modern Church has drifted far from this apostolic call.

- Repentance is minimized, turned into self-help or ignored altogether.

- Faith is reduced to a decision or mental agreement rather than true allegiance.

- Baptism is treated as optional or delayed until convenient.

- The Baptism of the Holy Spirit is confined to doctrine or denied altogether; the power promised has been neglected.

- The hope of His return is overshadowed by earthly distractions and preoccupations.

What has emerged in many places is a powerless Gospel—a message of forgiveness without transformation, decision without discipleship, invitation without expectation of the Spirit's power or the King's return.

But the Apostolic Gospel calls us back.

It summons the Church in this hour to:

- Recover the call to repentance—a radical turning from sin to God.

- Restore the call to faith—living allegiance to Jesus the risen King.

- Reclaim baptism as public identification with Christ and His people.

- Receive and walk in the Baptism of the Holy Spirit—power for witness, holiness, and mission.

- Rekindle the hope of His return—living in joyful, watchful expectancy.

Let us preach this Gospel with clarity. Let us respond to it with sincerity. Let us live it with urgency, as those who know that the King is coming soon.

Endnotes

1. Acts 2:38
2. Matthew 3:2; Matthew 4:17
3. Acts 17:30
4. Acts 26:20
5. Romans 10:9
6. Acts 2:41; Acts 8:36; Acts 16:33
7. Romans 6:3–4
8. 1 Peter 3:21
9. Acts 1:4–5
10. Acts 1:8
11. Acts 2:38–39
12. Joel 2:28–29
13. Ezekiel 36:25–27
14. Mark 16:20
15. 1 Thessalonians 1:10
16. 1 John 3:2–3

Chapter 6

THE DRIFT – A GOSPEL WE HAVE REPLACED

The tragic reality of church history is that, time and again, the Gospel the Apostles preached has been neglected, distorted, or replaced. Paul warned the Galatians with astonishment and sorrow:

"I am amazed that you are so quickly deserting Him who called you by the grace of Christ, for a different gospel; which is really not another; only there are some who are disturbing you and want to distort the gospel of Christ" (Gal. 1:6–7 NASB 1995).

The drift from the apostolic message is rarely sudden. It often happens subtly, a small deviation that over time leads the Church far from its foundation. What begins as an attempt to contextualize or to address cultural concerns can, if untethered from the Gospel, become a dangerous departure. In this chapter, we will examine how the Church has drifted into false gospels that replace the one true Gospel handed down by the Apostles.

A Gospel of Moralism

In some expressions of the Church, the Gospel has been reduced to a system of moral instruction—a call to be good, kind, and upright. The cross is presented as an example of self-sacrificial love rather than as the once-for-all atonement for sin. The resurrection is treated as an inspiring symbol of new beginnings rather than the historical inauguration of God's new creation.

This moralistic drift offers law without grace. It leaves people striving to do better without the power of the Holy Spirit. It produces either self-righteousness in those who feel they are succeeding or despair in those who know they are not. It speaks of ethics but not of the cross. It preaches improvement but not transformation.

A Gospel of Consumerism and Comfort

Elsewhere, the Gospel has been reshaped into a message of personal success, comfort, and well-being. The Kingdom of God is reduced to personal fulfillment. The promises of the Gospel are distorted to become guarantees of health, wealth, and happiness in this life. The message becomes one of self-actualization rather than self-denial.

This consumer gospel fills churches with spectators rather than disciples. It offers benefits without cost, crowns without crosses, and glory without suffering. It breeds entitlement rather than gratitude and leaves the Church indistinguishable from the world.

A Gospel of Cultural Accommodation

In an age that prizes tolerance above truth, many have reshaped the Gospel to fit the spirit of the age. Sin is redefined or ignored. The call to repentance is silenced lest it offend. The uniqueness of Christ as the only way of salvation is downplayed or denied in the name of inclusivity.

This drift empties the Gospel of its offense and, therefore, of its power. It makes peace with the world at the cost of faithfulness to Christ. It trades the power of the cross for the applause of culture. Paul's warning to Timothy rings true:

"For the time will come when they will not endure sound doctrine; but wanting to have their ears tickled, they will accumulate for themselves teachers in accordance to their own desires" (2 Tim. 4:3).

A Gospel Without Israel, Without the Kingdom, Without the King's Return

Perhaps most tragically, the Church has often forgotten the Gospel's connection to Israel's story, to the Kingdom of God, and to the return of the King. The Gospel is preached as if detached from the covenants, the promises, and the prophetic hope of Scripture. The Kingdom becomes internalized or spiritualized, and the glorious hope of Christ's return is neglected or ignored altogether.

When the Gospel is stripped of its eschatological edge and its covenantal roots, it loses its power to anchor the Church in hope and mission. The result is a Christianity preoccupied with the present world and unprepared for the age to come.

The Drift and the Call to Return

The drift from the apostolic Gospel has left the Church powerless where it should be powerful, compromised where it should be courageous, and silent where it should speak with prophetic authority. The only remedy is to return to the Gospel the Apostles preached.

We must return:

- To the Gospel of the Kingdom: the announcement that Jesus is Lord, the Messiah of Israel, the hope of the nations.

- To the Gospel of the cross: Christ crucified for sinners, the power and wisdom of God.

- To the Gospel of the resurrection: Christ raised, death defeated, the new creation begun.

- To the Gospel of the Spirit: Christ's people filled with power for mission and holiness.

- To the Gospel of the coming King: the world's true hope, the day of judgment, and the restoration of all things.

Let us repent of every false gospel we have embraced. Let us refuse the empty promises of moralism, consumerism, and cultural accommodation. Let us recover the bold, Christ-exalting, Spirit-empowered message that alone can save and sanctify. The Spirit is calling. The trumpet is sounding. It is time to return.

Endnotes

1. Galatians 1:6–7

2. 2 Timothy 4:3

Chapter 7

THE POWERLESS GOSPEL – WHERE IS THE SPIRIT?

The Gospel the Apostles preached was never a matter of words alone. It came in the power of the Holy Spirit. Paul testified to the Thessalonians,

"For our gospel did not come to you in word only, but also in power and in the Holy Spirit and with full conviction" (1 Thess. 1:5 NASB 1995).

When the Gospel is preached without the power of the Spirit, it loses its divine force. It becomes a matter of rhetoric, philosophy, or persuasion rather than the living word of God that confronts, convicts, and transforms. In this chapter, we will consider how the Church has drifted from the Spirit-empowered Gospel and what it means to return.

The Apostolic Gospel and the Power of the Spirit

From the beginning, the Apostolic Gospel was inseparable from the promise of the Spirit. Jesus commanded His disciples to wait in Jerusalem until they were clothed with power from on high (Luke 24:49). He promised,

"You will receive power when the Holy Spirit has come upon you; and you shall be My witnesses both in Jerusalem, and in all Judea and Samaria, and even to the remotest part of the earth" (Acts 1:8).

The outpouring of the Spirit at Pentecost was not an optional enhancement to the Gospel. It was the necessary empowerment for the mission of the Church. The Spirit's coming fulfilled the promise of the new covenant (Acts 2:16–18; Joel 2:28–29). The Spirit convicted the world of sin, righteousness, and judgment (John 16:8). The Spirit confirmed the word with signs following (Heb. 2:3–4). The Apostolic Gospel was always a Gospel of word and power.

The Drift from Spirit-Powered Gospel

Over time, many segments of the Church have drifted into a powerless gospel. This drift has taken various forms.

In some places, the promise of the Spirit has been confined to theological confession but denied in practice. The Church acknowledges the Spirit's role historically but no longer expects His power today. The Baptism of the Holy Spirit is treated as a doctrine of the past rather than an experience for the present.

In other contexts, the Spirit has been reduced to a private comforter rather than the One who empowers for bold witness. The Church seeks inspiration and consolation from the Spirit but neglects His call to mission, holiness, and demonstration of the Kingdom.

In still other places, the Spirit has been replaced by human strategies, programs, and performances. The Church looks to marketing, technology, and entertainment to accomplish what only the Spirit can do.

The result is a gospel without fire, without authority, and without the manifest presence of God.

The Signs of a Powerless Gospel

Where the Gospel has been stripped of the Spirit's power, several signs inevitably follow:

- The message loses its cutting edge. It no longer convicts of sin or calls sinners to repentance with authority.

- The Church becomes reliant on human effort rather than divine enabling.

- The supernatural works that confirmed the word in the apostolic era are absent or denied.

- The mission loses urgency, as the Spirit's passion for the nations fades from view.

- Holiness declines, for it is the Spirit who sanctifies.

A powerless Gospel produces powerless Christians—those who have a form of godliness but deny its power (2 Tim. 3:5).

The Call to Return

The Apostolic Gospel calls the Church to recover the promise, the power, and the presence of the Spirit:

- To preach not in word only, but in the demonstration of the Spirit and power (1 Cor. 2:4–5).

- To seek and receive the Baptism of the Holy Spirit, as the early Church did (Acts 2:4; Acts 4:31).

- To walk in the Spirit's fullness, bearing His fruit and exercising His gifts (Gal. 5:22–23; 1 Cor. 12:7–11).

- To depend upon the Spirit for mission, witness, and holiness.

The Gospel the Apostles preached is a Gospel of the cross, the resurrection, the Kingdom, and the Spirit. To return to this Gospel is to return to Pentecost—not as a one-time event, but as the continual empowerment of the Church for the age in which we live.

Let the Church hear what the Spirit is saying. Let us repent of our reliance on human strength. Let us seek again the promise of the Father and be clothed with power from on high.

Endnotes

1. 1 Thessalonians 1:5
2. Luke 24:49
3. Acts 1:8
4. Acts 2:16–18
5. Joel 2:28–29
6. John 16:8
7. Hebrews 2:3–4
8. 2 Timothy 3:5
9. 1 Corinthians 2:4–5
10. Acts 2:4
11. Acts 4:31
12. Galatians 5:22–23
13. 1 Corinthians 12:7–11

Chapter 8

THE CROSS REDUCED, THE RESURRECTION NEGLECTED

At the heart of the Gospel the Apostles preached stands the cross and the resurrection of Jesus Christ. Together, they are the power of God for salvation, the fulfillment of God's promises, and the foundation of the Church's hope. Yet in many places, the Church has drifted into a message that reduces the cross and neglects the resurrection. The result is a gospel emptied of its saving power.

Paul's words to the Corinthians remain as relevant today as when they were first written:

"For I determined to know nothing among you except Jesus Christ, and Him crucified" (1 Cor. 2:2 NASB 1995).

"And if Christ has not been raised, your faith is worthless; you are still in your sins" (1 Cor. 15:17).

The Reduction of the Cross

The Apostolic Gospel proclaims the cross as the once-for-all atonement for sin, the place where the justice and mercy of God meet, where the wrath of God is satisfied, and where sinners are reconciled to God. The cross is not merely an example of love; it is the altar on which the Lamb of God was slain for the sins of the world (John 1:29).

Yet in many quarters of the Church today, the cross has been reduced. It is presented as an inspiring symbol of self-sacrifice, a moral example to follow, or an emblem of suffering in solidarity with others. The message of substitutionary atonement—the heart of the cross—is muted or denied. The offense of the cross is removed, leaving a sanitized, domesticated symbol that no longer confronts sinners with their need for redemption.

Such a reduction produces a gospel of works rather than grace. It offers inspiration without salvation and comfort without cleansing. It leaves sinners unpardoned and the Church powerless.

The Neglect of the Resurrection

The Apostolic Gospel proclaims the resurrection as the vindication of Jesus as the Son of God, the firstfruits of the new creation, and the guarantee of the believer's future resurrection. The resurrection is not a spiritual metaphor or private hope. It is the historical, bodily triumph of God over death and the decisive beginning of His renewal of all things.

But in much modern preaching, the resurrection is neglected or emptied of its power. It is treated as a symbol of hope, a metaphor for new beginnings, or a myth to inspire moral living. Its historicity is downplayed. Its eschatological significance is ignored.

This neglect leaves the Gospel incomplete. Without the resurrection, the cross is a tragedy rather than a triumph. Without the resurrection, the Church has no living hope, no assurance of victory over death, no anchor for its future.

The Consequences of the Drift

When the cross is reduced and the resurrection neglected, the Gospel loses its power to save. A cross without atonement leaves sinners under condemnation. A resurrection without victory leaves death unconquered. A Church that preaches such a gospel will lack holiness, hope, and mission. It will substitute human effort for divine grace, and worldly optimism for the sure hope of eternal life.

Paul warns of such a drift:

"Having a form of godliness, although they have denied its power" (2 Tim. 3:5).

The Call to Return

The Apostolic Gospel calls us back to the cross and the resurrection as the center of our faith and proclamation:

- To the cross: Christ crucified, bearing the curse of the Law, satisfying divine justice, reconciling sinners to God (Gal. 3:13; Rom. 3:25–26; Col. 1:20).

- To the resurrection: Christ risen, death defeated, the firstfruits of those who sleep, the guarantee of the new creation (1 Cor. 15:20–23; Rom. 6:9; 1 Pet. 1:3).

We must preach Christ crucified and risen—not as moral example or myth, but as the historical, saving act of God. We must call sinners to the cross for cleansing, and we must hold forth the resurrection as the sure hope of glory.

Let the Church once again proclaim with power:

"He was delivered over because of our transgressions, and was raised because of our justification" (Rom. 4:25).

Endnotes

1. 1 Corinthians 2:2
2. 1 Corinthians 15:17
3. John 1:29
4. 2 Timothy 3:5
5. Galatians 3:13
6. Romans 3:25–26
7. Colossians 1:20
8. 1 Corinthians 15:20–23
9. Romans 6:9
10. 1 Peter 1:3
11. Romans 4:25

Chapter 9

A GOSPEL WITHOUT THE KING'S RETURN

The Gospel the Apostles preached was not only the proclamation of what Christ has done; it was the announcement of what Christ will do. It looked forward to the day when the risen Lord would return in glory to judge the living and the dead, to restore Israel, to establish His Kingdom in fullness, and to renew all things. This eschatological hope was not a peripheral doctrine—it was central to the message that turned the world upside down.

Paul declared to the philosophers at Athens:

"Therefore having overlooked the times of ignorance, God is now declaring to men that all people everywhere should repent, because He has fixed a day in which He will judge the world in righteousness through a Man whom He has appointed, having furnished proof to all men by raising Him from the dead" (Acts 17:30–31 NASB 1995).

The hope of the King's return shaped the Church's worship, fueled its mission, and sustained its endurance under trial. But in many parts of the modern Church, this hope has been neglected or marginalized. The Gospel has been preached as if the story is complete, as if the Kingdom has fully come, as if history has no climax beyond human progress or the individual's entrance into heaven.

The Apostolic Gospel and the Hope of His Appearing

From the beginning, the Apostolic Gospel was a message oriented toward the future. The angels at the ascension declared:

"This Jesus, who has been taken up from you into heaven, will come in just the same way as you have watched Him go into heaven" (Acts 1:11).

The Apostles taught that the return of Christ would bring:

- The resurrection of the dead (1 Cor. 15:22–23)

- The judgment of all people (2 Tim. 4:1)

- The restoration of Israel (Rom. 11:25–27)

- The renewal of creation (Acts 3:21; Rom. 8:19–21)

- The consummation of the Kingdom (1 Cor. 15:24–25)

This hope was not vague or symbolic. It was the sure expectation of Christ's personal, visible, bodily return to reign as King over all the earth.

The Drift from the Hope of His Return

Over time, many in the Church have lost this forward-looking vision. In some places, the return of Christ has been relegated to the realm of speculative theology, debated by scholars but ignored by the people of God. In other contexts, it has been spiritualized, treated as a metaphor for the triumph of good over evil or the believer's personal encounter with Christ at death.

In still other places, the Church has become so preoccupied with the present world—its comforts, its causes, its crises—that it has ceased to long for the coming of the King. The hope of His appearing has been eclipsed by lesser hopes: social progress, political solutions, or personal fulfillment.

This drift leaves the Church unprepared for the age to come. It weakens its witness, saps its courage, and diminishes its holiness. As John writes:

"Everyone who has this hope fixed on Him purifies himself, just as He is pure" (1 John 3:3).

The Consequences of Neglecting His Return

A Gospel without the King's return is a gospel without final justice, without the fulfillment of God's promises, without the restoration of creation. It leaves the world's great wrongs unrighted, death unconquered, and history without a glorious climax. It diminishes the urgency of repentance, the call to holiness, and the motivation for mission.

The Apostolic Gospel calls us to live as those "looking for the blessed hope and the appearing of the glory of our great God and Savior, Christ Jesus" (Titus 2:13).

The Call to Return

The Church must recover the eschatological hope that shaped the Gospel the Apostles preached:

- The hope of Christ's visible, bodily return
- The hope of the resurrection of the dead
- The hope of the restoration of Israel
- The hope of the renewal of all creation
- The hope of the consummation of the Kingdom

We must preach the Gospel not only as the message of what Christ has done but of what He will do. We must call the Church to watchfulness, readiness, and longing for the King's appearing.

Let the Church lift its eyes from the things of this world. Let us proclaim again with joy and urgency:

"He who testifies to these things says, 'Yes, I am coming quickly.' Amen. Come, Lord Jesus" (Rev. 22:20).

Endnotes

1. Acts 17:30–31
2. Acts 1:11
3. 1 Corinthians 15:22–23
4. 2 Timothy 4:1
5. Romans 11:25–27
6. Acts 3:21
7. Romans 8:19–21
8. 1 Corinthians 15:24–25
9. 1 John 3:3
10. Titus 2:13
11. Revelation 22:20

Chapter 10

RECOVERING THE GOSPEL OF THE KINGDOM

The first words of Jesus' public ministry were these:

"Repent, for the kingdom of heaven is at hand" (Matt. 4:17 NASB 1995).

The Kingdom was the central theme of Jesus' teaching. It was also the center of the Apostles' proclamation. Philip preached "the good news about the kingdom of God and the name of Jesus Christ" (Acts 8:12). Paul, in the final words recorded in the book of Acts, is described as "preaching the kingdom of God and teaching concerning the Lord Jesus Christ with all openness, unhindered" (Acts 28:31).

To recover the Gospel the Apostles preached, we must recover the Gospel of the Kingdom.

The Kingdom Announced

The Gospel of the Kingdom is the announcement that God's rule has broken into human history through the person of Jesus the Messiah. It is the proclamation that the King has come, that His authority has been established, and that the age to come has begun in the midst of this present evil age.

In the words of Jesus, "If I cast out demons by the Spirit of God, then the kingdom of God has come upon you" (Matt. 12:28). The signs, wonders, deliverances, and healings of Jesus were not mere proofs of compassion—they were the tangible evidence that the reign of God had arrived.

The Apostolic Gospel announced that the promises made to Israel—the promise of a Davidic King, a new covenant, and the restoration of all things—had begun to be fulfilled in Jesus of Nazareth.

The "Now and Not Yet" of the Kingdom

While the Kingdom has come in Christ's first coming, it has not yet come in fullness. The Kingdom was inaugurated in Jesus' ministry, but it will be consummated at His return. In this tension of the "already" and the "not yet," the Church lives and witnesses.

Jesus taught that the Kingdom is like a mustard seed—small in its beginning, yet destined to grow until it fills the earth (Matt. 13:31–32). It is like leaven—quiet, hidden, yet transforming everything it touches (Matt. 13:33). The Apostles preached the Kingdom as both a present reality and a future hope.

To recover the Gospel of the Kingdom is to proclaim this dual truth: the King reigns now, and He is coming again. His rule has been established in the hearts and lives of His people, and one day it will be visible over all the nations of the earth.

The Kingdom and Israel

The Kingdom of God cannot be rightly understood apart from Israel. Jesus is the Son of David, the heir to the throne of Israel. The Gospel proclaims that in Him, the promises made to the patriarchs have been fulfilled (Rom. 15:8). The Apostles never separated the Kingdom from the restoration of Israel.

Even after the resurrection, the disciples asked, "Lord, is it at this time You are restoring the kingdom to Israel?" (Acts 1:6). Jesus did not correct their theology—He corrected their timing: "It is not for you to know times or epochs which the Father has fixed by His own authority" (Acts 1:7). Their expectation was valid; its fulfillment would await His return.

To preach the Gospel of the Kingdom is to proclaim a future in which Israel will be restored and the nations will stream to Zion to learn the ways of the Lord (Isa. 2:2–4; Zech. 14:9).

The Kingdom and the Nations

The Gospel of the Kingdom is a global Gospel. It is not limited to Israel; it is for all nations. The King has come to rule over every tribe and tongue, and the Great Commission is the command to make disciples of all nations and teach them to obey everything He has commanded (Matt. 28:18–20).

This is not merely a mission of individual salvation—it is the expansion of the Kingdom of God on earth. It is the calling of people out of every nation into allegiance to the true King. The Apostolic Gospel creates a new humanity, united not by ethnicity or ideology, but by faith in Jesus and submission to His lordship.

The Kingdom and the Church

The Church is not the Kingdom, but it is the sign, agent, and instrument of the Kingdom in this age. It is the gathered people of the King, filled with the Spirit of the King, living under the reign of the King, bearing witness to the rule of the King.

To recover the Gospel of the Kingdom is to call the Church to live as a Kingdom people—distinct from the world, yet engaged in the world; holy in conduct, yet bold in witness; longing for His return, yet working faithfully until He comes.

The Call to Return

The Church must recover the Gospel of the Kingdom:

- A Gospel that announces the rule of God in Christ

- A Gospel that is rooted in the story of Israel

- A Gospel that proclaims salvation and lordship together

- A Gospel that demands repentance, allegiance, and discipleship

- A Gospel that looks forward to the day when the King returns to reign

Let us reject gospels that reduce the message of Jesus to personal improvement, cultural activism, or disembodied spirituality. Let us preach the Gospel of the Kingdom with power, clarity, and urgency. For the King reigns, and the King is coming.

Endnotes

1. Matthew 4:17
2. Acts 8:12
3. Acts 28:31
4. Matthew 12:28
5. Matthew 13:31–33
6. Romans 15:8
7. Acts 1:6–7
8. Isaiah 2:2–4
9. Zechariah 14:9
10. Matthew 28:18–20

Chapter 11

RECOVERING THE GOSPEL OF THE CROSS AND THE RESURRECTION

At the center of the Gospel the Apostles preached stand two great historical realities: the cross and the resurrection of Jesus Christ. Together, they form the heart of Christian proclamation and the foundation of Christian hope. Paul summarized the message this way:

"For I delivered to you as of first importance what I also received, that Christ died for our sins according to the Scriptures, and that He was buried, and that He was raised on the third day according to the Scriptures" (1 Cor. 15:3–4 NASB 1995).

To recover the Gospel the Apostles preached, we must recover the Gospel of the cross and the resurrection.

The Cross: Christ Crucified for Sinners

The Apostolic Gospel proclaims the cross not as a tragic end, but as the saving purpose of God. Jesus died "for our sins according to the Scriptures." He died as our substitute, bearing the punishment we deserved, fulfilling the Law's righteous requirement, and reconciling us to God. The cross is the altar on which the Lamb of God took away the sin of the world (John 1:29).

The cross is the wisdom of God and the power of God (1 Cor. 1:23–24). It silences human pride, exposes human sin, and reveals divine love. The Apostolic Gospel does not offer the cross as a moral example, an inspiring symbol, or a political statement. It proclaims the cross as the place where the wrath of God was satisfied and the grace of God was poured out.

To recover the Gospel of the cross is to recover the message that salvation is by grace alone, through faith alone, because of Christ alone. It is to reject every gospel of self-improvement, moralism, or works-righteousness.

The Resurrection: Christ Risen, Death Defeated

The Apostolic Gospel proclaims that the One who was crucified has been raised from the dead. The resurrection is not an optional addition to the cross; it is its necessary and glorious sequel.

"If Christ has not been raised, your faith is worthless; you are still in your sins" (1 Cor. 15:17).

The resurrection is the vindication of Jesus as the Son of God (Rom. 1:4). It is the declaration that His sacrifice was accepted. It is the firstfruits of the new creation (1 Cor. 15:20). It is the guarantee that death has been defeated and that all who belong to Christ will share in His victory.

To recover the Gospel of the resurrection is to recover the hope of glory—the sure and certain promise of the bodily resurrection of the dead, the renewal of creation, and the reign of Christ over all things.

The Cross and Resurrection as One Gospel

The Apostolic Gospel holds the cross and resurrection together. The cross without the resurrection would leave Jesus in the grave, His mission unfinished, and His followers without hope. The resurrection without the cross would leave sin unatoned, justice unsatisfied, and salvation impossible.

Together, the cross and resurrection declare that Jesus has conquered sin and death, that salvation has been accomplished, and that the age to come has broken into history.

The Call to Live the Gospel of the Cross and Resurrection

The Gospel of the cross and resurrection is not only to be preached; it is to be lived. The Apostolic Gospel calls believers to:

- Take up the cross, dying to sin and self (Luke 9:23; Gal. 2:20)
- Walk in the power of the resurrection, living as those raised to newness of life (Rom. 6:4)
- Bear witness to the crucified and risen Lord with boldness and joy (Acts 4:33)

To recover the Gospel of the cross and resurrection is to call the Church back to its foundation, to restore its hope, and to rekindle its mission.

The Call to Return

Let the Church proclaim again:

- Christ crucified: the Lamb of God who takes away the sin of the world.
- Christ risen: the firstborn from the dead, the Lord of life, the hope of glory.

Let us reject gospels that minimize the cross, neglect the resurrection, or reduce the Gospel to human effort or earthly gain. Let us preach and live the message that turned the world upside down:

"He was delivered over because of our transgressions, and was raised because of our justification" (Rom. 4:25).

Endnotes

1. 1 Corinthians 15:3–4
2. John 1:29
3. 1 Corinthians 1:23–24
4. 1 Corinthians 15:17
5. Romans 1:4
6. 1 Corinthians 15:20
7. Luke 9:23
8. Galatians 2:20
9. Romans 6:4
10. Acts 4:33
11. Romans 4:25

Chapter 12

RECOVERING THE GOSPEL OF THE SPIRIT AND THE COMING KING

The Gospel the Apostles preached was a Gospel of power and of promise. It was the good news that through the death, resurrection, and ascension of Jesus, the age of the Spirit had dawned, and that the King who came in humility would return in glory to reign over all the earth. The Church today must recover this Gospel—the Gospel of the Spirit and the coming King.

The Gospel of the Spirit

From the day of Pentecost, the Apostolic Gospel was proclaimed not in word only, but in demonstration of the Spirit and of power (1 Cor. 2:4). The outpouring of the Spirit was not a side note to the Gospel—it was the fulfillment of God's promise and the evidence that the Messiah had been exalted. Peter declared:

"Therefore having been exalted to the right hand of God, and having received from the Father the promise of the Holy Spirit, He has poured forth this which you both see and hear" (Acts 2:33 NASB 1995).

The Gospel of the Spirit is the Gospel of the new covenant, in which God gives His people new hearts and puts His Spirit within them so that they may walk in His ways (Ezek. 36:26–27). It is the Gospel of power for witness, holiness, and mission. It is the Gospel of the Kingdom advancing not by might, nor by power, but by the Spirit of the Lord (Zech. 4:6).

To recover this Gospel is to call the Church back to:

- Expect and seek the Baptism of the Holy Spirit (Acts 1:5; Acts 2:4)

- Depend on the Spirit's power for mission and ministry (Acts 1:8)

- Walk in the Spirit's fullness, bearing His fruit and exercising His gifts (Gal. 5:22–23; 1 Cor. 12:7–11)

The Gospel of the Coming King

The Apostolic Gospel was not only the proclamation of Christ crucified, risen, and ascended; it was the announcement that the King would come again. The return of Jesus was the Church's blessed hope, the fulfillment of God's promises to Israel, and the consummation of the Kingdom.

Paul wrote:

"We wait for His Son from heaven, whom He raised from the dead, that is Jesus, who rescues us from the wrath to come" (1 Thess. 1:10).

The Gospel of the coming King declares that:

- Christ will return visibly, bodily, and in glory (Acts 1:11)

- He will judge the living and the dead (2 Tim. 4:1)

- He will restore Israel and reign over the nations (Rom. 11:26–27; Zech. 14:9)

- He will renew creation, making all things new (Acts 3:21; Rev. 21:5)

This hope fuels the Church's holiness, sustains its mission, and anchors its endurance.

"Everyone who has this hope fixed on Him purifies himself, just as He is pure" (1 John 3:3).

The Call to Return

To recover the Gospel the Apostles preached is to recover:

- The Gospel of the Spirit: Christ's people empowered for mission, sanctified by the Spirit, and living in dependence on His presence

- The Gospel of the coming King: the announcement of the return of Jesus, the judgment of the nations, and the restoration of all things

Let us reject gospels that deny the Spirit's power, that abandon the hope of His appearing, or that reduce the Gospel to private spirituality or present comfort. Let the Church be renewed by the Gospel of the Spirit and the coming King—the Gospel that announces:

"The Spirit and the bride say, 'Come.' And let the one who hears say, 'Come.'" (Rev. 22:17).

Endnotes

1. 1 Corinthians 2:4
2. Acts 2:33
3. Ezekiel 36:26–27
4. Zechariah 4:6
5. Acts 1:5
6. Acts 2:4
7. Acts 1:8
8. Galatians 5:22–23
9. 1 Corinthians 12:7–11
10. 1 Thessalonians 1:10
11. Acts 1:11
12. 2 Timothy 4:1
13. Romans 11:26–27
14. Zechariah 14:9
15. Acts 3:21
16. Revelation 21:5
17. 1 John 3:3
18. Revelation 22:17

Chapter 13

RETURNING TO APOSTOLIC PRACTICES

The Gospel the Apostles preached was not a set of abstract truths. It created a community shaped by the Word of God, empowered by the Spirit, and marked by practices that reflected the reign of Christ. The book of Acts describes not only what the Apostles proclaimed but how they lived. To return to the Gospel they preached is also to return to the practices their Gospel produced.

The Devotion of the Apostolic Church

The early believers devoted themselves to the apostles' teaching, to fellowship, to the breaking of bread, and to prayer.[1] These practices were not optional extras. They were the natural outworking of faith in the crucified and risen Christ and the indwelling of the Holy Spirit. The Church was a learning church, a worshiping church, a praying church, and a loving community.[2]

Fellowship and Generosity

The Apostolic Church was marked by generosity and shared life. All who believed were together, sharing what they had, and meeting the needs of the community.[3] This was not forced collectivism, but the fruit of hearts transformed by grace. There was not a needy person among them, for those who owned property sold it to provide for others.[4] True fellowship (koinonia) involved both spiritual communion and practical care.[5]

Worship and the Lord's Supper

The early Church worshiped together, both in the temple courts and from house to house, breaking bread with gladness and sincerity of heart.[6] The Lord's Supper was central to their gatherings—a proclamation of the Lord's death until He comes, a participation in His body and blood, and a foretaste of the coming Kingdom.[7]

Mission and Witness

The Apostolic Church was a missionary church. They received power when the Holy Spirit came upon them and became witnesses to Jesus to the ends of the earth.[8] With great power the Apostles gave testimony to the resurrection of the Lord Jesus, and great grace was upon them all.[9] They proclaimed the Gospel publicly, made disciples of all nations, and ministered in the power of the Spirit.[10] They rejoiced to suffer for His name.[11]

Leadership, Discipline, and Community Life

The Apostolic Church appointed elders in every church, men who shepherded the flock willingly and as examples to the flock.[12] The community was marked by mutual submission, accountability, and loving discipline to protect its purity.[13] Leaders kept watch over the souls entrusted to their care, knowing they would give an account.[14]

The Call to Return

To return to the Gospel the Apostles preached is to return to the practices their Gospel produced:

- A people devoted to the Word, prayer, and worship
- A fellowship marked by generosity, hospitality, and love

- A mission-driven community empowered by the Spirit

- A body led by faithful shepherds, walking in holiness, and waiting for the return of the King

Let the Church devote itself again to the Apostolic pattern, so that the world may see and know that Jesus is Lord.

Endnotes

1. Acts 2:42

2. Acts 6:4; 1 John 1:7

3. Acts 2:44–45

4. Acts 4:34–35

5. Romans 12:13; Hebrews 13:16

6. Acts 2:46–47

7. 1 Corinthians 10:16; 1 Corinthians 11:23–26

8. Acts 1:8

9. Acts 4:33

10. Acts 5:42; Acts 8:4; Matthew 28:19–20; Mark 16:20

11. Acts 5:41; 2 Timothy 3:12

12. Acts 14:23; 1 Peter 5:1–4

13. Acts 5:1–11; 1 Corinthians 5:1–13

14. Hebrews 13:17

Conclusion

THE CLARION CALL

The Gospel the Apostles preached was a message of divine power, rooted in God's covenant faithfulness, centered on the cross and resurrection, filled with the Spirit's presence, and oriented toward the coming of the King. It was a Gospel that confronted sin, offered grace, announced the Kingdom, and summoned all people everywhere to repent and believe. It was the Gospel that turned the world upside down.

Yet in every generation—including our own—the Church is tempted to drift. We substitute moralism for the cross, consumerism for the Kingdom, accommodation for repentance, and human strategies for the power of the Spirit. We preach a gospel of forgiveness without transformation, hope without holiness, and Christ without His crown.

But the trumpet is sounding. The Spirit is calling. The clarion call goes forth: Return.

Return to the Gospel of the Kingdom—the announcement that Jesus is Lord, the Son of David, the hope of Israel and the nations.

Return to the Gospel of the cross—Christ crucified for sinners, the Lamb of God who takes away the sin of the world.

Return to the Gospel of the resurrection—Christ risen, death defeated, the firstfruits of the new creation.

Return to the Gospel of the Spirit—the power of God for witness, holiness, and mission.

Return to the Gospel of the coming King—the blessed hope of the Church, the promise of justice, the restoration of Israel, and the renewal of all things.

This is the Gospel that saves. This is the Gospel that sanctifies. This is the Gospel that will prepare the Bride for the coming of the Bridegroom.

Closing Charge

Let the Church hear and heed the call. Let preachers preach it. Let believers live it. Let the Gospel the Apostles preached be the Gospel we proclaim until the King returns. May we stand in that day, having been faithful stewards of the message entrusted to us.

"Therefore, my beloved brethren, be steadfast, immovable, always abounding in the work of the Lord, knowing that your toil is not in vain in the Lord" (1 Cor. 15:58 NASB 1995).

Amen. Even so, come, Lord Jesus.

Appendix A

KEY SCRIPTURES OF THE APOSTOLIC GOSPEL

The Gospel as the Fulfillment of God's Promises

- Genesis 12:1–3 — God's covenant with Abraham: "In you all the families of the earth will be blessed."

- 2 Samuel 7:12–13 — God's covenant with David: "I will raise up your descendant after you... and I will establish the throne of his kingdom forever."

- Isaiah 9:6–7 — The promised ruler from David's line: "The government will rest on His shoulders... His kingdom will have no end."

- Luke 1:31–33 — The angel's announcement: "The Lord God will give Him the throne of His father David... His kingdom will have no end."

- Romans 15:8–9 — "Christ has become a servant to the circumcision on behalf of the truth of God to confirm the promises given to the fathers."

The Kingdom of God

- Matthew 4:17 — "Repent, for the kingdom of heaven is at hand."

- Matthew 12:28 — "If I cast out demons by the Spirit of God, then the kingdom of God has come upon you."

- Luke 4:43 — "I must preach the kingdom of God... for I was sent for this purpose."

- Acts 1:3 — "[Jesus] spoke of the things concerning the kingdom of God."

- Acts 8:12 — "Philip... was preaching the good news about the kingdom of God and the name of Jesus Christ."

- Acts 28:31 — "Preaching the kingdom of God and teaching concerning the Lord Jesus Christ with all openness, unhindered."

- Daniel 7:13–14 — "His dominion is an everlasting dominion which will not pass away; and His kingdom is one which will not be destroyed."

The Cross: The Atoning Death of Jesus

- Isaiah 53:5–6 — "He was pierced through for our transgressions... the LORD has caused the iniquity of us all to fall on Him."

- John 1:29 — "Behold, the Lamb of God who takes away the sin of the world!"

- Romans 3:25–26 — "God displayed [Christ] publicly as a propitiation in His blood through faith... so that He would be just and the justifier of the one who has faith in Jesus."

- 1 Corinthians 1:23–24 — "We preach Christ crucified, to Jews a stumbling block and to Gentiles foolishness, but to those who are the called... the power of God and the wisdom of God."

- 1 Corinthians 15:3 — "Christ died for our sins according to the Scriptures."

- Galatians 3:13 — "Christ redeemed us from the curse of the Law, having become a curse for us."

- Colossians 1:20 — "Through Him to reconcile all things to Himself, having made peace through the blood of His cross."

The Resurrection: Victory over Death

- Psalm 16:10 — "You will not abandon my soul to Sheol; nor will You allow Your Holy One to undergo decay."

- Matthew 28:6 — "He is not here, for He has risen, just as He said."

- Acts 2:32 — "This Jesus God raised up again, to which we are all witnesses."

- Romans 1:4 — "[Christ] was declared the Son of God with power by the resurrection from the dead."

- Romans 6:9 — "Christ, having been raised from the dead, is never to die again; death no longer is master over Him."

- 1 Corinthians 15:20–23 — "Christ has been raised from the dead, the first fruits of those who are asleep… in Christ all will be made alive."

- 1 Peter 1:3 — "He has caused us to be born again to a living hope through the resurrection of Jesus Christ from the dead."

The Outpouring and Work of the Spirit

- Joel 2:28–29 — "I will pour out My Spirit on all mankind… I will pour out My Spirit in those days."

- Ezekiel 36:26–27 — "I will put My Spirit within you and cause you to walk in My statutes."

- Matthew 3:11 — "[Jesus] will baptize you with the Holy Spirit and fire."

- Acts 1:8 — "You will receive power when the Holy Spirit has come upon you; and you shall be My witnesses."

- Acts 2:4 — "They were all filled with the Holy Spirit and began to speak with other tongues."

- Acts 2:33 — "Having received from the Father the promise of the Holy Spirit, He has poured forth this which you both see and hear."

- 1 Corinthians 12:7–11 — "But to each one is given the manifestation of the Spirit for the common good… distributing to each one individually just as He wills."

The Return of the King and the Restoration of All Things

- Isaiah 2:2–4 — "In the last days… the law will go forth from Zion… He will judge between the nations."

- Zechariah 14:9 — "The Lord will be king over all the earth."

- Acts 1:11 — "This Jesus… will come in just the same way as you have watched Him go into heaven."

- Acts 3:21 — "[Heaven] must receive [Christ] until the period of restoration of all things."

- Romans 11:25–27 — "The Deliverer will come from Zion, He will remove ungodliness from Jacob."

- 1 Thessalonians 1:10 — "We wait for His Son from heaven… who rescues us from the wrath to come."

- Titus 2:13 — "Looking for the blessed hope and the appearing of the glory of our great God and Savior, Christ Jesus."

- Revelation 21:5 — "Behold, I am making all things new."

- Revelation 22:20 — "Yes, I am coming quickly. Amen. Come, Lord Jesus."

The Call to Respond

- Isaiah 55:6–7 — "Seek the Lord while He may be found... let the wicked forsake his way."

- Mark 1:15 — "The time is fulfilled, and the kingdom of God is at hand; repent and believe in the gospel."

- Acts 2:38 — "Repent, and each of you be baptized in the name of Jesus Christ for the forgiveness of your sins; and you will receive the gift of the Holy Spirit."

- Romans 10:9–10 — "If you confess with your mouth Jesus as Lord, and believe in your heart that God raised Him from the dead, you will be saved."

- Luke 9:23 — "If anyone wishes to come after Me, he must deny himself, and take up his cross daily and follow Me."

- Acts 17:30–31 — "God is now declaring to men that all people everywhere should repent, because He has fixed a day in which He will judge the world in righteousness."

Notes

This list is not exhaustive of all Scripture, but it provides a rich foundation for proclaiming, studying, and praying the Gospel as the Apostles preached it. Each passage reflects key themes of the book:

covenant fulfillment, the Kingdom of God, the atoning cross, the victorious resurrection, the empowering Spirit, the coming King, and the call to respond in repentance and faith.

Appendix B (Supplement)

COMPARATIVE CHART OF KEY APOSTOLIC SERMONS IN ACTS

The book of Acts records the Apostolic Gospel in action. The sermons of Peter, Stephen, Paul, and others provide the earliest examples of how the Gospel of the Kingdom, the cross, the resurrection, the Spirit, and the coming King was proclaimed. The following charts represents foundational proclamations of that message.

Sermon	Audience	Main Christological Claims	Core Proclamation	Call to Respond
Acts 2 (Pentecost)	Jews and proselytes in Jerusalem	Jesus is Lord and Christ; crucified and raised from the dead	Fulfillment of prophecy; outpouring of the Spirit; resurrection of Jesus	Repent, be baptized, receive the Spirit
Acts 3 (Solomon's Portico)	Jews at the temple	Jesus is God's Servant; Author of life raised by God	God's fulfillment of covenant promises; restoration to come	Repent, return, so sins may be wiped away
Acts 10 (Cornelius' house)	Gentiles (God-fearers)	Jesus anointed by the Spirit; judge of the	Peace through Jesus; death and resurrection;	Believe in Him

		living and the dead	forgiveness of sins	
Acts 13 (Pisidian Antioch)	Jews and God-fearers in synagogue	Jesus is the promised Savior from David's line	Fulfillment of covenant; crucifixion and resurrection; justification by faith	Believe for forgiveness
Acts 17 (Areopagus)	Gentile philosophers (Athenians)	Jesus as risen Man appointed to judge the world	God the Creator commands repentance; resurrection proof of coming judgment	Repent

Old Testament Citations and Allusions in Key Apostolic Sermons

Sermon	Old Testament Citations / Allusions	Purpose in Sermon
Acts 2	Joel 2:28–32; Psalm 16:8–11; Psalm 110:1	Proves Spirit outpouring and resurrection of the Messiah
Acts 3	Deuteronomy 18:15–19; Genesis 22:18; Genesis 12:3; Genesis 26:4; Genesis 28:14	Affirms Jesus as the Prophet like Moses; covenant fulfillment
Acts 10	Isaiah 53 (implicit allusion); Psalm 118:22 (stone rejected, though not quoted)	Highlights suffering Servant and universal salvation

Acts 13	Psalm 2:7; Isaiah 55:3; Psalm 16:10; Habakkuk 1:5	Declares Jesus as Son; resurrection proof; warning to heed
Acts 17	Genesis 1–2 (Creator God); Isaiah 42:5 (implied)	Establishes God as Creator and judge

Notes for Study

- The sermons in Acts consistently proclaim Jesus as the fulfillment of Israel's Scriptures — whether preaching to Jews steeped in the Law and Prophets or to Gentiles unfamiliar with them.

- Psalm 16 and Psalm 110 are central texts for demonstrating Jesus' resurrection and exaltation.

- The call to respond is always grounded in the reality of what God has done in Christ: repent, believe, be baptized, receive the Spirit, and await His return.

Appendix C

THE GOSPEL IN THE EPISTLES – SUMMARY OF APOSTOLIC TEACHING

The epistles of the New Testament unfold the Apostolic Gospel in greater depth, explaining its meaning, implications, and demands. They present the same message proclaimed in Acts: the Gospel of the Kingdom, the cross, the resurrection, the Spirit, and the hope of the coming King. The following summary highlights the core elements of this Gospel as taught across the epistles.

The Gospel as the Fulfillment of God's Promises

- Romans 1:1–4 — The Gospel concerns God's Son, born of the seed of David, declared the Son of God with power by the resurrection from the dead.

- Galatians 3:8 — Scripture preached the Gospel beforehand to Abraham: "All the nations will be blessed in you."

- 2 Corinthians 1:20 — All the promises of God are "Yes" in Christ.

The Apostolic Gospel teaches that Jesus fulfills God's covenant promises to Israel and brings blessing to the nations.

The Gospel Proclaims Christ Crucified

- 1 Corinthians 1:23–24 — We preach Christ crucified, the power of God and the wisdom of God.

- Galatians 3:13 — Christ redeemed us from the curse of the Law by becoming a curse for us.

- Romans 3:25–26 — God displayed Christ as a propitiation through His blood, demonstrating His righteousness.

- Colossians 1:20 — Christ made peace through the blood of His cross.

The cross is central as the means of atonement, reconciliation, and victory over sin.

The Gospel Declares the Resurrection

- 1 Corinthians 15:3–4 — Christ died for our sins, was buried, and was raised on the third day according to the Scriptures.

- Romans 6:9 — Christ, having been raised from the dead, is never to die again; death no longer is master over Him.

- 1 Peter 1:3 — God has given us new birth into a living hope through the resurrection of Jesus Christ.

The resurrection is both the vindication of Jesus and the assurance of the believer's future resurrection.

The Gospel Is the Power of the Spirit

- Romans 8:9–11 — The Spirit who raised Jesus from the dead dwells in believers and gives life.

- Galatians 3:14 — The blessing of Abraham comes to the Gentiles so that we might receive the promise of the Spirit through faith.

- 1 Corinthians 12:7 — To each one is given the manifestation of the Spirit for the common good.

The Gospel includes the promise of the Spirit, empowering believers for holy living, mission, and unity.

The Gospel Calls for Faith, Repentance, and Obedience

- Romans 10:9–10 — If you confess with your mouth Jesus as Lord, and believe in your heart that God raised Him from the dead, you will be saved.

- Galatians 2:20 — The life I now live in the flesh I live by faith in the Son of God.

- Titus 2:11–14 — The grace of God instructs us to deny ungodliness and worldly desires and to live sensibly, righteously, and godly.

The Apostolic Gospel calls not only for belief but for an ongoing life of allegiance, obedience, and holiness.

The Gospel Announces the Coming King

- 1 Thessalonians 1:10 — We wait for His Son from heaven, Jesus, who rescues us from the wrath to come.

- Philippians 3:20–21 — We eagerly wait for a Savior, the Lord Jesus Christ, who will transform our body of humility into conformity with His body of glory.

- 2 Timothy 4:1 — Christ Jesus, who is to judge the living and the dead, and by His appearing and His Kingdom.

The Gospel points forward to the visible, bodily return of Jesus Christ, the final judgment, and the renewal of all things.

Summary

The Apostolic teaching in the epistles presents the Gospel as the fulfillment of God's covenant, the proclamation of Christ crucified and risen, the means of salvation through grace and faith, the power of the Spirit for holy living, and the hope of the coming King. This Gospel alone is the power of God for salvation to everyone who believes.

Appendix D

RECOMMENDED READING FOR FURTHER STUDY

On the Kingdom of God

George Eldon Ladd, The Gospel of the Kingdom

Though not Pentecostal, Ladd's work has profoundly influenced Pentecostal and Charismatic theology of the Kingdom of God. Ladd explores the "already and not yet" nature of the Kingdom, emphasizing its present reality through Christ's ministry and its future consummation at His return. His framework provides a biblical foundation for Spirit-empowered Kingdom mission.

Frank D. Macchia, Jesus the Spirit Baptizer: Christology in Light of Pentecost

Macchia, a leading Pentecostal theologian, presents a Christ-centered theology that integrates the Kingdom of God and the Baptism in the Holy Spirit. He shows how Pentecost completes the saving work of Jesus, empowering the Church for Kingdom mission.

On the Cross and Resurrection

Gordon D. Fee, Paul, the Spirit, and the People of God

Fee offers a deeply Trinitarian and Pentecostal reading of Paul's letters, showing how the cross, resurrection, and Spirit are inseparably linked in God's plan of redemption. This accessible work invites believers to live in the dynamic power of the Spirit made possible by Christ's atoning work.

Stanley M. Horton, The Cross and Salvation: The Doctrine of Salvation

Horton provides a Pentecostal systematic treatment of salvation, rooted in the cross and resurrection. He emphasizes both the legal (justification) and transformative (sanctification, Spirit empowerment) aspects of salvation, reflecting a Spirit-filled soteriology.

On the Holy Spirit

R. A. Torrey, The Baptism with the Holy Spirit

Torrey's classic work helped shape the early Pentecostal and Charismatic movements. He argues from Scripture for the necessity of the Baptism in the Holy Spirit as an empowering experience for Christian witness and holy living, distinct from conversion.

Stanley M. Horton (ed.), What the Bible Says About the Holy Spirit

This volume offers a comprehensive Pentecostal exposition of the person and work of the Holy Spirit, including the Spirit's role in regeneration, sanctification, spiritual gifts, mission, and eschatology. It remains a standard reference in Pentecostal seminaries.

On the Return of Christ

J. Rodman Williams, Renewal Theology: God, the World, and Redemption (Vol. 1–3)

Williams, a prominent Charismatic scholar, presents a full systematic theology that integrates orthodox Trinitarian doctrine with Spirit-filled renewal themes. His sections on eschatology and the return of Christ affirm both the future hope of the King's return and the Spirit's work in preparing the Church for that day.

Robert H. Gundry, The Church and the Tribulation

Although Gundry was not Pentecostal, this classic work remains one of the most thorough and scholarly defenses of the post-tribulation rapture position. It offers detailed exegesis of key texts (especially Matthew 24, 1 Thessalonians 4, and Revelation) and emphasizes the Church's endurance through tribulation. Widely respected across Spirit-filled and evangelical circles for its rigorous biblical argument.

Marvin J. Rosenthal, The Pre-Wrath Rapture of the Church

Rosenthal's work presents a pre-wrath, post-tribulational perspective that has been influential among many Charismatic and Pentecostal believers seeking to harmonize the hope of Christ's return with the biblical testimony of the Church's suffering. His book challenges both pre-tribulational and mid-tribulational frameworks with careful biblical analysis.

Stanley M. Horton, Our Destiny: Biblical Teachings on the Last Things

While Horton doesn't enter extensive debate about rapture timing, his Assemblies of God eschatology leans toward a post-tribulational framework, emphasizing the visible, bodily return of Christ after a time of great tribulation. He focuses on the unity of Christ's second coming event rather than a secret rapture.

On the Gospel and Mission

David Wesley Myland, The Latter Rain Covenant

Myland, one of the earliest Pentecostal theologians, explores the connection between Spirit outpouring, the Gospel of the Kingdom, and the mission of the Church in the last days. His work reflects early Pentecostal expectation of revival and global harvest.

Melvin L. Hodges, The Indigenous Church

Hodges offers a practical theology of missions from a Pentecostal perspective. He emphasizes Spirit-empowered, indigenous-led churches as the goal of biblical missions, reflecting a Kingdom model of evangelization that depends on the Spirit's work rather than human control.

Notes on the List

- All these works reflect a Trinitarian theology.

- All affirm or significantly contribute to a Pentecostal or Charismatic understanding of Scripture, mission, and eschatology.

- The list includes both foundational classics and scholarly works suitable for pastors, students, and leaders seeking to recover and proclaim the Gospel the Apostles preached.

www.ingramcontent.com/pod-product-compliance
Lightning Source LLC
Chambersburg PA
CBHW060533030426
42337CB00021B/4237